CROSS WORD

PUZZLES

FOR CLEVER Kids

TRIP PAYNE

JUNIOR

PUZZLE WRIGHT JUNIOR New York

An Imprint of Sterling Publishing Co., Inc.
1166 Avenue of the Americas
New York, NY 10036

This Puzzlewright Junior edition published in 2017.
The puzzles in *Crossword Puzzles for Clever Kids* are taken from:
Crosswords for Kids
© 1999 by Trip Payne
Great Crosswords for Kids
© 2002 by Trip Payne

ISBN 978-1-4549-2482-1

Distributed in Canada by Sterling Publishing
c/o Canadian Manda Group, 664 Annette Street
Toronto, Ontario, Canada M6S 2C8
Distributed in the United Kingdom by GMC Distribution Services
Castle Place, 166 High Street, Lewes, East Sussex, England BN7 1XU
Distributed in Australia by NewSouth Books, 45 Beach Street, Coogee,
NSW 2034, Australia

For information about custom editions, special sales, and premium and
corporate purchases, please contact Sterling Special Sales at 800-805-5489
or specialsales@sterlingpublishing.com.

Manufactured in Canada
Lot #:
2 4 6 8 10 9 7 5 3 1
05/17

www.sterlingpublishing.com
www.puzzlewright.com

CONTENTS

INTRODUCTION

IF YOU'VE NEVER TRIED SOLVING a crossword puzzle before, it's just like playing a video game, except that it's a lot less noisy, and there's not as much action . . . and there's no controller either. Well, okay, maybe it's not like a video game at all. Forget I said that.

The puzzles in this book are filled with things that you probably know a lot about—games, food, school, sports, music, and so on. There might be a word now and then that you don't know. Just remember, it's not "cheating" to ask someone else for help when you get stuck. In fact, it's a good way to learn something new. (And some of these words come up more than once, so after you learn them the first time, you can guess them by yourself the next time!)

I hope you enjoy this book of video games . . . I mean, this book of crossword puzzles!

—*Trip Payne*

ACROSS

1 Rice Krispies sound
4 Little round vegetable
7 Drink that's often "sweetened" or "unsweetened"
10 Square section of a window
11 Not feeling well
12 Sixty-minute periods: Abbreviation
13 Joe Biden, for example: 2 words
16 "Planet of the ___"
17 Card that can be worth 1 or 11
18 Continent that contains Mount Everest
19 ___ Talks (lectures by experts)
20 A man might wear one with a suit
21 Guide a car
22 Prince William, to Prince Charles
23 Dessert with a crust
24 City in Montana
27 "I've ___ an idea!"
28 Not cooked at all
31 "Peekaboo, ___ you!": 2 words
32 Opposite of "peace"
33 The North ___ (where Santa lives)

34 Where the person at 13-Across works: 3 words
37 Two times five
38 "You ___ My Sunshine"
39 4 goes ___ 12 three times
40 2016 and 2017, for example: Abbreviation
41 Not "no" or "maybe"
42 Color Easter eggs

DOWN

1 Walked back and forth nervously
2 Dollar bills that show George Washington
3 Energy and enthusiasm
4 Slice
5 "What ___ could I do?"
6 Boxer nicknamed "The Greatest"
7 The ones over here
8 Bert's roommate on "Sesame Street"
9 "When you wish upon ___ ...": 2 words
10 Lead ___ (weapon in the game Clue)
13 Container that stores dye

14 Weather that would spoil a picnic

15 July 4, 1776, for example

20 It's at the end of the foot

21 Stop standing

22 Food that contains meat and vegetables

23 Very tiny hole in the skin

24 Itty-___ (very tiny)

25 Person who shows people to their seats

26 People between 12 and 20 years old

27 Bill ___ (the founder of Microsoft)

28 Path that a mail carrier travels

29 Not to mention

30 Very small

32 Some fences are made of it

33 ___ express (old mail delivery system)

35 It's scattered around in barns

36 Put something where it wouldn't be found

ACROSS

1 Birds that are often blue
5 Close friend
8 What omelets are made of
12 Black-and-white cookie
13 Put frosting on a cake
14 Kind of song sung in 29-Across
15 Alexander Graham ___ (inventor of the telephone)
16 It's used to catch fish
17 Pressed the doorbell
18 Not first
20 State where Nashville is: Abbreviation
22 Opposite of "tall"
24 "Little Miss Muffet sat on a tuffet, eating ___ curds and whey"
25 Dachshund or Dalmatian
28 "___ now, brown cow?"
29 "Carmen" is a famous one
31 ___ ball (the white ball in pool)
32 What nodding your head means
33 Truck that moves furniture
34 Intelligent
36 Now and ___

38 Strap that's used to control a horse
39 "Go away!"
41 Animal that's like a big monkey
43 Use a keyboard
46 Put clothes away in the closet
47 What a boy will become
48 You have ten of them on your body
49 You have two of them on your body
50 An aardvark might eat one
51 Make a noise with your thumb and middle finger

DOWN

1 Career
2 "___ You There God? It's Me, Margaret" (Judy Blume book)
3 National park in Wyoming
4 ___ eclipse
5 Half of a quart
6 High card in a suit
7 Q, for example
8 Deserve
9 National park in Arizona: 2 words

10 ___ rummy (card game)
11 Droop
19 Appliance in the kitchen
21 Get chalk off the blackboard
22 Afraid to meet new people
23 A gardener uses it to attack weeds
24 Bird on a farm
26 Your and my
27 Obtain
30 Country that has a famous canal

35 Baseball catchers wear them
37 Big pigs
38 Money paid to the landlord
39 That woman
40 Farmers might put it into a bale
42 Frying ___
44 "The Princess and the ___"
45 Power that psychics say they have: Abbreviation

ACROSS

1 Cain's brother, in the Bible

5 Put ___ show: 2 words

8 "___ Loves You" (Beatles song)

11 Harry Potter does it

13 Scary rodent

14 Item in a Happy Meal

15 It's sometimes on top of a Christmas tree

16 Long ___ (way back when)

17 Animal that mates with a ram

18 "Yield" or "Don't Walk," for example

20 Average score on a golf course

22 Alphabet's beginning

25 "Family Guy" daughter

26 Allows

29 Beverage that uses ice cream: 3 words

33 Go from one house to a new one

34 Yankees manager Girardi

35 Secret agent

36 Finish

38 Its capital is Salt Lake City

40 Candy ___

42 "Aladdin" prince

44 Dish of tossed vegetables

48 What metal is called when it has just been mined

49 Hanukkah's month, usually: Abbreviation

50 Copy a drawing

51 Place for napping

52 Observe

53 Changes the color of one's hair

DOWN

1 "Today I ___ man" (bar mitzvah boy's phrase): 2 words

2 Forbid

3 It might be hard-boiled

4 Doesn't tell the truth

5 Beverage at breakfast: 2 words

6 Old horse

7 Above

8 Music systems

9 "___ do you do?"

10 Where the pupil is

12 Go up a ladder

19 "___ whiz!"

21 100 percent

22 It's attached to the shoulder

23 Ghosts say it

24 ___ wagon (pioneer's transportation)

27 Sound that a woodpecker makes

28 Where a pig lives

30 Bill that has a portrait of Alexander Hamilton on it

31 Decay

32 Big dinner

37 Fathers

39 Really tough

40 ___ for apples (what you might do on Halloween)

41 "___ you serious?"

43 Robert E. ___ (general in the Civil War)

45 Put down

46 Quick tennis point

47 ___ Moines (capital of Iowa)

ACROSS

1 Play a kazoo
4 Person who makes up rhymes
8 Unit of computer memory
12 Every once ___ while: 2 words
13 "Hey, what's the big ___?"
14 Thin as a ___ (very skinny)
15 Game with deeds and Chance cards
17 "Excuse me …"
18 "Little Bo-Peep has lost ___ sheep …"
19 Pocket fuzz
21 Word you use during long division
24 You make soup in it
25 Sound of a ray gun
28 Rescue a car
29 Constellations are made up of them
31 Animal that gives birth to lambs
32 "___ was saying …": 2 words
33 Baby goat
34 Vehicle that can handle rough terrain
35 Part of the leg
37 Sticky stuff

39 "___'s Dragon" (2016 Disney film)
41 Game with tiles and Triple Letter Squares
46 "And they lived happily ___ after"
47 Fix mistakes in writing
48 Younger version of the word at 3-Down
49 "What ___ we thinking?"
50 Part of a camera
51 Take someone to court

DOWN

1 "All of the other reindeer used to laugh and call ___ names …"
2 Numero ___ (#1)
3 Guy
4 Frosty the Snowman had one
5 Bad smell
6 Long, skinny fish
7 Singer Swift
8 Ingredient in some cereals that has a lot of fiber
9 Game with dice and "small straights"
10 Make a knot
11 Kind of tree
16 Exclamation like "Aha!"

20 "___ none of your business!"

21 "Give ___ chance!": 2 words

22 1, 2, and 3: Abbreviation

23 Game with colored circles and a spinner

24 Lily ___ (what a frog sits on)

26 In ___ of (impressed by)

27 ___ rally

29 Glide down a snowy mountain

30 Shiny stuff on a Christmas tree

34 What someone does for a living

36 In this spot

37 Smile broadly

38 Grains that horses eat

39 Long seat in church

40 Christmas ___ (December 24)

42 Letters between B and F

43 Ammo for a toy gun

44 "Skip to My ___"

45 Private ___ (detective)

ACROSS

1 Insect that lives in a hill
4 Opposite of "skinny"
7 Sack
10 Game that ends in a tie score
11 Not wild
12 A long time ___
13 Electronic device in the living room: 2 words
16 A half plus a half
17 Drenches with water
18 Part of a parka
19 Parts of quarts: Abbreviation
20 ___ and outs
21 Put in the mail
22 Covered in frost
23 "What's the reason?"
24 Adorable
26 Black-eyed ___ (little vegetable)
27 Animal that moos
30 "That's terrible!": 2 words
31 Smack in the face
32 King Kong was one
33 Electronic device in the kitchen: 2 words
36 Sick

37 Walking stick
38 Some people pay it every month
39 Peg that golfers use
40 Explosive stuff: Abbreviation
41 Suffix after "host" or "lion"

DOWN

1 "You ___ the boss of me!"
2 Barry, Harry, and Larry
3 16-Across plus 16-Across
4 Truthful bits of information
5 Famous ___ (brand of cookie)
6 3-Down times five
7 The Red ___ (Snoopy's enemy)
8 "Merry Christmas to all, and to all ___ night!": 2 words
9 Valuable metal
10 Let something fall
11 ___-weeny
14 More than once

15 All those people
21 Rectangle or square
22 "Believe ___ not!": 2 words
23 Make something with a loom
24 Country in South America
25 Member of the family
26 It grows in a garden

27 Homes for bats
28 Unlocks
29 Left the room
30 Leave out
31 What the Ugly Duckling turned into
34 Halloween's month: Abbreviation
35 State that's next to Idaho: Abbreviation

ACROSS

1 Part of the ear where you put an earring
5 Tie a shoe
9 It can cool you off in the summer
12 "Now ___ me down to sleep ...": 2 words
13 "Today I am ___" (bar mitzvah boy's declaration): 2 words
14 ___ de Janeiro, Brazil
15 ___ Wazowski (monster in "Monsters University")
16 Part of a three-piece suit
17 It can end the words "count" and "priest"
18 Cain and Abel's mother
19 Part of a robe
20 ___ child (kid with no brothers or sisters)
21 Fix a magazine story
23 Meeting where people try to talk to ghosts
25 A limerick, for example
27 "Get ___ the program!"
28 Fake hair to hide baldness
30 Part of a barn where hay is stored
32 Funny people
33 Snoozes
35 Kylo ___ (character in "Star Wars: The Force Awakens")
37 "___ Yankee Doodle Dandy": 2 words
38 "In ___ of emergency, break glass"
39 ___ and dandy
40 "Have we ___ somewhere before?"
41 High cards, usually
42 More or ___
43 Athlete who gets paid
44 A karate student wears one
45 Takes advantage of

DOWN

1 Jell-O flavor
2 Salad ingredient, perhaps
3 Common side dish: 2 words
4 Hole in a needle
5 What a volcano shoots
6 Make ___ of things (foul things up): 2 words
7 Kidney-shaped nut
8 It can end the word "differ"

9 Common side dish: 2 words

10 What a bride walks down

11 Like a snoop

19 A ___ in the right direction

20 "Hold ___ your hat!": 2 words

22 Papers given to people who lend money: Abbreviation

24 Is sick

26 "Dennis the ___"

28 Stopwatch, for example

29 It holds up a painter's canvas

31 Stressed out

32 Cowardly person

34 Gnat or flea, for example

36 Suffix for "quick" or "thick"

38 Vehicle that people "hail" when they want it

39 Sickness that's common in winter

ACROSS

1 "___ tell you what …"
4 Word on a light switch
7 Points found on some wire fences
12 Drink that's sometimes "iced"
13 Bath place
14 "Take ___ at this!": 2 words
15 It's celebrated in late winter: 3 words, abbreviation
18 "___ making a list" (lyric from "Santa Claus Is Coming to Town")
19 Name for a lion
20 "Could you do me a ___?"
23 Mayonnaise holder
24 A trapeze artist might fall into it
27 Run ___ from home
28 Short sleep
29 Word on a valentine
30 Room that might have a TV in it
31 Do some needlework
32 Noisemaker on an ambulance
33 The Civil ___
34 Music from Drake
35 It's celebrated in early spring: 3 words

42 A good employee might get one
43 Overweight
44 Ginger ___
45 Uses a keyboard
46 Commercials
47 What wrestlers wrestle on

DOWN

1 "___ up to you"
2 Permit
3 One time around the track course
4 Mammal that likes to play in water
5 Mink and ermine
6 Crime-fighting group with a list of the 10 most-wanted fugitives: Abbreviation
7 "The butcher, the ___, the candlestick maker"
8 Not to mention
9 Fishing pole
10 ___ constrictor (big snake)
11 It's up above us
16 Word a sailor says instead of "Hello!"
17 Applaud

20 Popular thing that doesn't last long
21 Amazement
22 Martin ___ Buren (former president)
23 Bone that enables you to chew
24 Word that goes with "neither"
25 She lived in the Garden of Eden
26 What X is equal to, in Roman numerals
28 Brand name of "soft" balls
29 You kiss with them
31 Department store events
32 Sprinkles a certain seasoning on food
33 Very smart
34 Street
35 Paintings and so forth
36 Give money to
37 Make a tear in
38 Three ___ kind (poker hand): 2 words
39 A beaver builds it
40 State next to Georgia: Abbreviation
41 Up to now

ACROSS

1 Dog, cat, or hamster, for example
4 Emergency letters
7 Jewish religious leader
12 "I ___ you one!"
13 Wolf down
14 Tim ___ (actor who voiced Buzz Lightyear)
15 Comic strip created by Charles M. Schulz
17 Football team in Detroit
18 Suffix for "heir"
19 "___ sesame!"
20 Walks in water
23 Word that Scrooge said
24 When the sun is out
27 ___ rain (ecology problem)
28 Miles ___ hour
29 Have a nice meal
30 Kind of toothpaste
31 What groceries are put into
32 You pull them out of a garden
33 It comes at the end of a restaurant meal
35 You need it for frying
36 Birds that fly in a V shape
38 Comic strip created by Bill Amend

42 Monsters in fairy tales
43 Get older
44 "What ___ you talking about?"
45 Carries
46 ___ and reel
47 Ballpoint ___

DOWN

1 The sound a balloon makes
2 Female sheep
3 The Mad Hatter drank it
4 Dr. ___ (children's book author)
5 Some grains
6 Roads: Abbreviation
7 "Wreck-It ___" (Disney movie)
8 Tell ___ (fib): 2 words
9 Comic strip created by Chic Young
10 Big ___ (famous landmark in London)
11 Drive-___ (places where movies are watched from cars)
16 Require
19 It helps row a boat
20 What a dog's tail might do

21 Highest-ranked card in a suit
22 Comic strip created by Scott Adams
23 Plead
25 Hide-___-seek
26 Word of agreement
28 Good friend
29 Result of a minor traffic accident
31 "___ you!" (reaction to a sneeze)
32 Polished the floor
34 "Peekaboo, ___ you!": 2 words
35 ___ stick (bouncy toy)
36 "You've ___ to be kidding"
37 What a conceited person has a lot of
38 Distant
39 Kind of music Kanye West makes
40 Raw metal
41 A dozen minus a pair

ACROSS

1 Against the ___ (illegal)
4 Read electronically
8 Scoop water out of a boat
12 "A long time ___ ..."
13 Mexican food
14 Muppet on "Sesame Street" who has a goldfish named Dorothy
15 Snakes
17 Mountains in Europe
18 Kids sometimes sit on Santa's ___
19 Music store purchases, for short
20 "___ and the Tramp"
22 Wild pig
25 Money that's left for the waiter
28 "___ my pleasure"
29 Easter animal
30 Part of a royal flush, in poker
31 It holds up a golf ball
32 Word said at the end of a prayer
33 The people who work on a boat
34 Little ___ Riding Hood
36 As easy as falling off a ___

37 What umbrellas protect you from
39 Not forward or backward
44 Like cars that aren't new
45 Hot thing in the kitchen
46 "Oh, give ___ home where the buffalo roam ...": 2 words
47 Kind of fish
48 Stoop down
49 Finish up

DOWN

1 ___ Vegas
2 How old you are
3 Big baseball event: 2 words
4 A single stair
5 Soup comes in it
6 Play a role
7 Digits: Abbreviation
8 Small round thing on a necklace, sometimes
9 Big baseball event: 2 words, hyphenated
10 Little devil
11 ___ Angeles
16 Take care of the bills
19 Go "boo-hoo"

Crossword Grid

1	2	3	■	4	5	6	7	■	8	9	10	11
12			■	13				■	14			
15			16					■	17			
■		18				■		19			■	■
20	21			■	22	23	24		■	25	26	27
28			■	29				■		30		
31			■	32			■	33				
■		34	35			■		36			■	■
37	38			■	39	40	41				42	43
44				■	45				■	46		
47				■	48				■	49		

20 Turned on a lamp
21 Had some food
22 ___ around (wander aimlessly)
23 Half of two
24 Raggedy ___ (famous doll)
26 Cubes in the freezer
27 Where people sit in church
29 Opposite of "good"
33 Milk-giving animal
35 Finishes

36 Give money temporarily
37 ___ the wrong way (irritate)
38 "___ matter of fact ...": 2 words
39 Go "boo-hoo"
40 "___ Been Working on the Railroad"
41 Comfortable room of the house
42 Kind of money that's used in Japan
43 Not happy

ACROSS

1 Boxer's punches
5 Iggy Azalea's music
8 Big wooden pole on a ship
12 Words of understanding: 2 words
13 Suffix that means "most"
14 ___ Jazz (NBA team)
15 Disney movie
17 Not early
18 "What ___ doing here?": 2 words
19 Health resort
21 "___ the season to be jolly ..."
24 "Oh, what's the ___?" ("What difference does it make?")
26 Vegetable that makes you cry when you chop it
30 Stuff in a pen
31 Look without blinking
33 Number in a duo
34 Perhaps
36 Decay
37 Do what Betsy Ross was famous for doing
38 Commercials
40 Get ready to shoot a basketball
42 Not quite hot
45 Disney movie
50 Someone who lives in the Middle East
51 "___ got an idea!"
52 Final
53 Prefix for "colon" or "final"
54 Homer's neighbor on "The Simpsons"
55 Potatoes have them

DOWN

1 Brand of peanut butter
2 Red ___ beet: 2 words
3 Actor Affleck who played Batman in "Batman v Superman: Dawn of Justice"
4 ___ good example (what a role model should do): 2 words
5 "I couldn't ___" ("I just had to do it")
6 "Do ___ say!": 2 words
7 School groups that have open houses: Abbreviation
8 Disney movie
9 One ___ time: 2 words
10 Got into a chair
11 Most commonly written word in English

16 Made other people laugh
20 Like something written in verse
21 Tiny ___ (character in "A Christmas Carol")
22 "Never ___ million years!": 2 words
23 Where clouds are
25 Hearing organ
27 "___ been real!" ("I've had fun!")
28 Homophone of "oh"
29 At this moment
32 Sounded like a lion
35 Disney movie
39 ___ guards (protection for soccer players)
41 Stubborn animal
42 The past tense of "is"
43 "___ You Smarter Than a 5th Grader?"
44 Male sheep
46 New Year's ___
47 ___ an egg (flop)
48 Ending for "Japan" or "Vietnam"
49 Roads: Abbreviation

ACROSS

1 Villain in "The Lion King"
5 It's near your waist
8 What a spider spins
11 Triangle or trapezoid
12 Portland's state: Abbreviation
13 Pie ___ mode: 2 words
14 Bedsheet material
15 Werewolf or vampire
17 They invade picnics
18 Famous male doll
19 Quick kiss
20 Vegetable that comes in a pod
21 ___ conditioning
22 Line you make in your hair
23 Opposite of "first"
25 What Old MacDonald had
26 ___ 'n' roll
27 Light brown
28 Small magical being
31 Go sightseeing
32 Neat as a ___
33 Run away from
34 He had "new clothes" in a famous story

36 By yourself
37 Southern general Robert E. ___
38 Number that changes on your birthday
39 Makes repairs
40 ___ Angeles
41 Indicate "yes" with your head
42 Throw a football

DOWN

1 Polish
2 Juicy fruits
3 Big hairy animals
4 Kylo ___ (son of Han Solo)
5 Bart Simpson's father
6 Get wrinkles out of clothes
7 It contains ink
8 Juicy fruits
9 Vote into office
10 The outside of a tree
11 Hit with an open hand
16 Practice boxing

18 Box that contains the parts for a model car

21 Pose a question

22 "Peter ___"

24 Measure of land

25 It can cool down a room

26 "___ and Juliet"

27 Exhausted

29 Gives temporarily

30 Extra costs

31 William ___ (legendary archer who shot an apple off his son's head)

32 ___ stick (toy you hop on)

33 Bug that annoys dogs

35 Sprinted

36 Device that a guitar can be hooked up to

ACROSS

1 Makes knots
5 Place for a baby
9 Colored stripe in a hairdo
12 Kind of self-defense
14 Country with a famous canal
15 Did as you were told
16 Metal used to make cans
17 It's sometimes worth more than a king
18 Places where scientists work
21 Young woman, in slang
23 Leader of the Catholic Church
27 "You ___ here" (words on a mall map)
28 Pie ___ mode (pie with ice cream): 2 words
29 Come in first
30 Food that has meat and vegetables in it
32 Bone in the chest
33 You can ride downhill on it
34 "A long time ___, in a galaxy far, far, away …"
36 Munch on
38 Music system for the home

41 Tribe that Geronimo belonged to
45 Last name of the fictional detective Sherlock
46 ___ on (depends on)
47 Sweet potatoes
48 What Aladdin rubbed

DOWN

1 Measurement in a recipe: Abbreviation
2 "Give ___ rest!": 2 words
3 Ending for "north" or "south"
4 Chairs
5 Nasty person
6 ___ of light
7 Suffix for "meteor"
8 Garden plot
10 "What ___ doing here?": 2 words
11 Australian animals
12 Australian animal: 2 words
13 Easy as ___
18 ___ Vegas, Nevada
19 Museums show it
20 Spelling ___ (school competition)

22 Boxer known as "The Greatest"

24 Bird that comes out at night

25 As American as apple ___

26 "Dead ___" (street sign)

31 Heats

33 Delay

35 "Golly!"

37 Kind of animal Tarzan hung out with

38 Not eager to meet new people

39 Come ___ conclusion (decide): 2 words

40 Kind of tree

42 Organization that hires spies: Abbreviation

43 It's at the bottom of a pants leg or skirt

44 Supposedly, it's a "sixth sense": Abbreviation

ACROSS

1 ___ eagle (American symbol)
5 Not good
8 What you fill a bird feeder with
12 "Believe ___ not!": 2 words
13 Word that's shouted at a bullfight
14 Square part of a window
15 Some kids collect them: 2 words
18 Two-player card game
19 Boy
20 Owns
23 Things that attempt to sell products
25 Tattles
29 On the peak of
31 Depressed
33 Canvas thing on a boat
34 Where Houston is
36 Marry
38 Secret agent
39 Answer to an addition problem
41 Your lungs need it
43 What quarterbacks play in: 2 words

50 One of the five Great Lakes
51 A score of 3 to 3, for example
52 Place for a pet canary
53 Not sick
54 That girl
55 Side of a knife

DOWN

1 A baby wears it during meals
2 "I'm ___ loss for words!": 2 words
3 ___ Angeles
4 Made a sketch
5 Two-by-fours
6 "___ aboard!"
7 "The Farmer in the ___"
8 One of the four card suits
9 In one ___ and out the other
10 Go off the deep ___
11 ___ Moines, Iowa
16 Sheep's sound
17 Garfield is one
20 Head covering
21 Swallowed

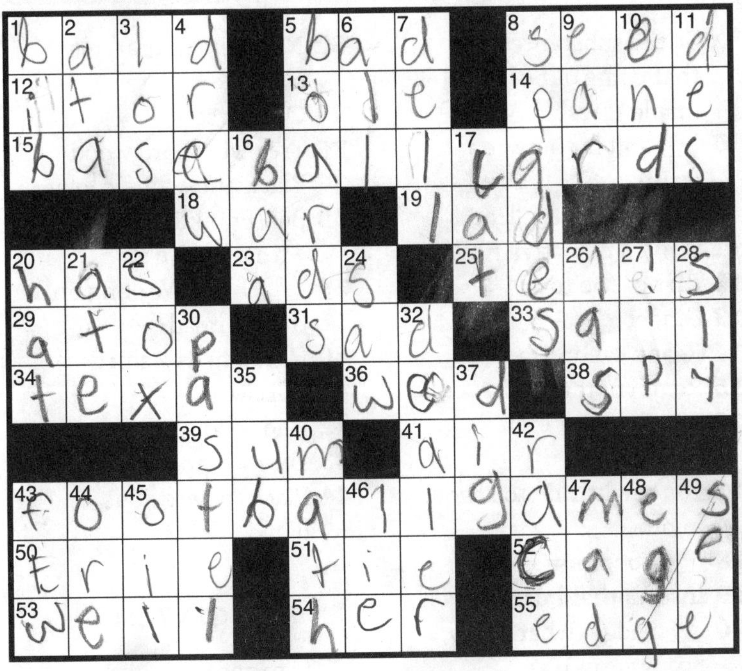

22 The Boston Red ___
24 Carpenter's cutter
26 ___ Vegas
27 It might get chapped
28 Sneaky, like a fox
30 Chalk-like crayon
32 Person who works in a casino
35 Vehicle that shoots torpedoes, for short
37 Use a shovel
40 School subject
42 The Indianapolis 500 is one
43 Not many
44 What miners try to find
45 Black fuel
46 Tell a whopper
47 Angry
48 "Which came first, the chicken or the ___?"
49 Observe

ACROSS

1 Sticky substances that come out of maple trees

5 ___ and far between (rare)

8 "The ___ in the Hat"

11 What a detective finds

12 Part of the foot

13 Ginger ___

14 Ready, willing, and ___

15 Remove from office

16 ___ the knot (get married)

17 You might ride to school in one

18 ___ hoop (kind of toy)

19 Insects that buzz

20 ___ badge (what a Boy Scout earns)

22 Find out new things in school

24 Stuff in a fireplace after a fire

25 Truck that moves furniture

26 Sharp and biting, like autumn weather

28 Fight

31 Stuff with fiber that's in healthy cereals

32 Numbers that aren't evens

34 Old horse

36 Tree with hard wood

37 Black-and-white cookie

38 Ben Franklin flew one with a key on it

39 "___ Been Working on the Railroad"

40 Have on, as a shirt

41 Thing

42 Had followers

43 Young man

44 Places where lions live

DOWN

1 It forms over a cut

2 Photo ___ (place to paste pictures)

3 Throbbing that you can feel near your wrist

4 Take a look at

5 Not fair, in baseball

6 Country in Central America: 2 words

7 Not dry

8 Provide the food for a party

9 Someone who flies in a flying saucer
10 Pegs used on a golf course
12 Country in Asia: 2 words
18 Sound a snake makes
19 Sound a firecracker makes
21 It can spoil a picnic
23 Prominent parts of a Mickey Mouse hat

26 Atlanta baseball player
27 Gathered the leaves in the yard
29 Bring together
30 Devoured
31 Put in hot water
33 Not alive
35 Jewels
37 Bird that hoots
38 Someone who's not a grownup yet

15

ACROSS

1 ___ Ruth (great baseball player)
5 Curly, like hair
9 Precious stone
12 "I smell ___!" ("Something is suspicious!"): 2 words
13 Big test
14 Word that can go before "lobe" or "ring"
15 Money you owe someone else
16 How much a dime is worth: 2 words
18 "You bet!"
20 Middle ___ (when someone isn't really young or really old)
21 Be a thief
23 Pump ___ (lift weights)
27 Hold tightly
30 Wedding vow: 2 words
31 They hold money and valuable papers
33 Happy ___ clam: 2 words
34 Strong smell
36 Opening in a fence
37 Camel's color
38 Angry
40 "___ was saying ...": 2 words
42 Cold drink: 2 words

47 Noisemaker in a car
50 It comes after "neither"
51 Mother ___ (kids' game): 2 words
52 "Hold ___ your hats!": 2 words
53 Billboards
54 Drove faster than the law allows
55 Animals that wear a yoke

DOWN

1 Terrible
2 "___ You There God? It's Me, Margaret" (Judy Blume book)
3 People born between 1946 and 1965: 2 words
4 Suffix for "disk" or "major"
5 Damp
6 Hatchet
7 Lucy ___ Pelt (character in "Peanuts")
8 One place to go to the gym: Abbreviation
9 People born in the 1960s and 1970s: 2 words
10 Have a meal
11 Wife's title: Abbreviation

17 What a chicken lays
19 Brother's sibling, for short
21 ___ Grande (river in Texas)
22 Weird
24 Dusting cloth
25 "This is the chance ___ lifetime!": 2 words
26 You need one in order to play badminton
28 "A mind ___ terrible thing to waste": 2 words
29 You fry bacon in it

32 Large body of water
35 Not cooked
39 They hold back rivers
41 "Go away!"
42 ___ good mood (happy): 2 words
43 Food fish
44 Poke someone on the shoulder
45 Homophone of "I"
46 Get ___ of (eliminate)
48 Highway: Abbreviation
49 Prefix for "sense" or "stop"

ACROSS

1 "The Red Planet"
5 One day ___ time: 2 words
8 Conversation
12 State where Toledo is
13 Kylo ___ (movie role for Adam Driver)
14 Sister of Bart Simpson
15 Bundles of paper
16 Enemy of Batman
18 "Just ___!" (Nike's slogan): 2 words
20 Use a needle and thread
21 Good buddy
23 Small bite
25 Enter data for a computer
29 People shout it to the bullfighter
30 Scrub really hard
32 Ending for "Japan"
33 Winter coat
35 Conclusion
36 Palindromic nickname for a girl
37 "Jack ___ Jill"
39 ___ Island (part of New York)
41 Enemy of Batman: 2 words, abbreviation

45 Uncle's wife
48 Part for an actor
49 They're not yeses
50 Chest protectors for babies
51 Graceful bird
52 Letters that signal for help
53 Metal fastener

DOWN

1 Clean the floor
2 "I knew it!"
3 Enemy of Batman
4 Just okay: Hyphenated
5 Ocean near the North Pole
6 Drink that's made from leaves
7 Little bugs
8 Class ___ (student who jokes around a lot)
9 That guy
10 White ___ sheet: 2 words
11 Slightly brown
17 Strange person
19 Crazy
21 "___ Goes the Weasel"

22 ___ mode (with ice cream): 2 words

24 Edgar Allan ___ (famous writer)

26 Enemy of Batman

27 Country between Canada and Mexico: Abbreviation

28 Number of arms on a squid

31 "Don't do anything ___ I tell you to"

34 Girl's name

38 Comfortable rooms in houses

40 Captures

41 ___ Potts ("Beauty and the Beast" character)

42 Move a canoe

43 Miami's state: Abbreviation

44 Place to see animals

46 Steph Curry's group: Abbreviation

47 ⅓ of a tablespoon: Abbreviation

ACROSS

1 Piece of paper taken to the supermarket
5 Gorillas
9 Blind as a ___
12 China's continent
13 Evil octopus in "Penguins of Madagascar"
14 "Who do you think you ___?"
15 Detective in kids' books: 2 words
17 Stan who makes cameo appearances in Marvel movies
18 Make a hole
19 A ___ apple: 2 words
20 Plot
21 Animal with antlers
23 Pressure
25 Grand finale
27 It's used to make maple syrup
28 Where Topeka is
31 Not far away
34 Roly-___ (round)
35 Emotional state
37 Cindy-___ Who (girl in "How the Grinch Stole Christmas!")
39 State near Washington: Abbreviation
40 Detectives in kids' books: 2 words
42 Revolutions ___ minute
43 Got older
44 "___ upon a time ..."
45 Have some food
46 Untidy place
47 They collect nectar

DOWN

1 ___ of Enchantment (New Mexico's nickname)
2 "Did you hear what ___?": 2 words
3 Burn a little bit
4 Tic-___-toe
5 Totals
6 Capital of France
7 Happenings
8 Do needlework
9 A game of pool uses 15 of them
10 Places
11 Someone between 12 and 20 years old
16 Materials that people knit with

20 ___ Le Pew (cartoon skunk)

22 "___, meeny, miny, moe ..."

24 "The Princess and the Frog" songwriter Newman

26 Harm

28 Asian country divided into "North" and "South"

29 Red ___ (danger signal)

30 Tender, achy spots

32 Without help

33 Rolls-___ (fancy car)

34 Vatican City religious leader

36 Evens' opponent in choosing up sides

38 ___ one's head (thinks)

40 Kind of meat

41 Actor Saget of "Fuller House"

ACROSS

1 Baseball hats
5 "___ your age and not your shoe size!"
8 Way to make money in the summer
11 Once more
13 An archer uses one
14 Go ___ diet (try to lose weight): 2 words
15 Fun ride: 2 words
18 "Glee" actress ___ Michele
19 Tell a fib
20 Doctors: Abbreviation
23 What might be served with potato chips
25 More recent
29 Sound that is made when a magician makes something disappear
31 "Do ___ disturb"
33 Like grass, in the morning
34 What to say when you answer the phone
36 ___ Sawyer (Huckleberry Finn's friend)
38 Black-and-yellow insect
39 ___ and downs
41 Used to be

43 Where you can ride the thing at 15-Across: 2 words
50 ___ and don'ts
51 Basketball player Hibbert
52 "___ makes waste"
53 Be in debt
54 How old you are
55 All those people

DOWN

1 Automobile
2 "Give it ___!" ("Try it!"): 2 words
3 Good friend
4 Part of a window
5 Network that shows "Dancing With the Stars"
6 Somewhat cold
7 Mark ___ ("Huckleberry Finn" author)
8 Write down quickly
9 Small number
10 Candy ___
12 Require
16 It can delay a baseball game
17 It can grow into a plant
20 55 ___ (speed limit): Abbreviation

21 Female deer
22 Note between fa and la
24 Cooking vessel
26 "Charlotte's ___"
27 Female sheep
28 Kind of bread
30 Winter sicknesses
32 Small city
35 Soap ___ (TV show that's on in the afternoon)
37 Algebra, for example
40 Weather problem

42 Small argument
43 "Much ___ About Nothing" (play by Shakespeare)
44 Cut the grass
45 "___ your imagination!"
46 Place for a contact lens
47 What's left after something burns
48 The path a mail carrier takes: Abbreviation
49 It fits into a lock

ACROSS

1 "___ in!" ("Eat up!")
4 Start of the alphabet
7 Light ___
11 Once ___ blue moon: 2 words
12 "Tra ___" (song sounds): 2 words
14 Thought
15 "Where the Wild Things Are" author: 2 words
18 Extra large or small, for example
19 Opposite of "love"
20 Ending for "Japan" or "Siam"
21 Look through a book
23 Sticky stuff used to make a road
24 Cherry-colored
25 Allow
27 Tear
29 Part of an atlas
32 Mauna ___ (volcano in Hawaii)
34 Has breakfast
37 Birmingham's state: Abbreviation
38 Big brass instrument
40 The ___ Piper
42 Author who wrote books about Busytown: 2 words

45 ___-ball (game where you roll balls)
46 Diamonds or hearts, for example
47 The first woman in the Bible
48 His and ___
49 ___ Vegas
50 ___ Moines, Iowa

DOWN

1 Turns down the lights
2 "The bombs bursting ___" (part of "The Star-Spangled Banner"): 2 words
3 Bandage material
4 Name of the prince in the movie "Aladdin"
5 Johann Sebastian ___ (famous composer)
6 Spike on the bottom of a soccer shoe
7 Container for coal
8 Part of a cow
9 Rent
10 Made a cake
13 "When you wish upon ___ ...": 2 words
16 Actual

17 Strange and spooky
22 One of the big airlines
26 Goes around and sees the sights
28 Father
29 Swampy area
30 "Share and share ___"
31 Indiana basketball player
33 Kareem ___-Jabbar (all-time leading scorer in the NBA)

35 Ready to go to sleep
36 Put food on the table
39 Where Russia and Japan are
41 They can change your hair color
43 "For ___ a jolly good fellow ..."
44 A quarter equals 25 of them: Abbreviation

ACROSS

1 Tear open
4 You pound them into the ground to anchor a tent
8 Fifty-yard dash, for example
12 ___ of a kind (unique)
13 Farm animals
14 "Now ___ me down to sleep ...": 2 words
15 Brownish color
16 Expensive automobile
18 Person who makes verses
20 "___ your imagination!"
21 The American flag has 50 of them
23 School group: Abbreviation
24 Gave a meal to
27 What golfers aim for
28 That guy's
29 Fly high
30 Positive answer
31 Weather that makes it hard to see
32 Fragments
33 What we breathe
34 What new parents have to decide on
35 Expensive automobile: 2 words
39 Rip ___ Winkle

42 Come to a stop
43 Direction on a compass
44 What a vain person has
45 Finishes
46 Stick around
47 One of the primary colors

DOWN

1 Decay
2 ___ little while (soon): 2 words
3 Faraway people you write to: 2 words
4 The north and south ends of the Earth
5 The way out
6 Sapphire or ruby, for example
7 Hogs' noses
8 "___ and shine!"
9 ___ Baba
10 "You ___ do it!"
11 Where the pupil and cornea are
17 ___ Today (popular newspaper)
19 Its capital is Salem: Abbreviation
21 Bashful

Across / Down clues:

22 Digit on the foot
23 Animal that gives us pork
24 Always
25 Consume
26 Medical workers: Abbreviation
28 They neigh and whinny
29 Froot Loops toucan
31 Physically ___ (in shape)
32 Birthday ___
33 ___ and crafts

34 Group that sends up space shuttles: Abbreviation
35 Pronoun for a girl
36 Peter ___ (boy who didn't want to grow up)
37 Not young
38 Popular pet
40 What candles on a birthday cake represent
41 Move your head up and down in agreement

ACROSS

1 Sinks downward
5 Supposed ability to read minds: Abbreviation
8 Cool ___ cucumber: 2 words
11 Sign above a door, sometimes
12 Thin as a ___
14 Corny joke
15 "If it ___ up to me ..."
16 Zoo animal
18 "Planet of the ___"
20 ___ shoes (things a ballerina wears)
21 Not on
23 The square root of 100
25 They're sold by the dozen
29 Barking sound
30 Stuffed-___ pizza
33 Big tree
34 Sandwich breads
36 Pekoe is a type of this
37 Baseball statistic: Abbreviation
38 Sam-___ (Dr. Seuss character): Hyphenated
41 Me, myself, ___: 2 words
43 Zoo animal
47 Too
50 "___ and improved"

51 Captain Hook's sidekick in "Peter Pan"
52 Cole ___ (common side dish)
53 Opposite of "live"
54 Put two and two together
55 Detest

DOWN

1 Join with stitches
2 The Tin Man carried one
3 Zoo animal
4 A ___ in the right direction
5 One end of a pencil
6 ___ Francisco
7 Movie star Brad ___
8 "Many years ___ ..."
9 It comes out of maple trees
10 Ending for "orphan" or "percent"
13 Zodiac sign that comes after Cancer
17 Grant's opponent in the Civil War
19 "And others": Abbreviation

1	2	3	4		5	6	7		8	9	10
11					12			13	14		
15					16				17		
		18		19			20				
21	22			23		24			25	26	27	28
29				30			31	32	33		
34			35			36			37		
		38	39	40		41		42			
43	44	45				46			47		48	49
50				51					52		
53				54					55		

21 Paddle for a boat

22 Cook in hot oil

24 Cashew or macadamia

26 Zoo animal

27 Talk and talk and talk

28 Water-___ (have fun on a lake)

31 "Please be ___" ("Get in your chairs")

32 Light brown color

35 Take a tiny drink of

39 Sounds the doctor tells you to make

40 One of the Berenstain Bears

42 Hundred-yard ___ (kind of race)

43 Conclusion

44 Ring of flowers they give out in Hawaii

45 She gives birth to a lamb

46 Boy's name

48 Weekend day: Abbreviation

49 "I ___ you one!" ("I'm in your debt!")

ACROSS

1 They connect things to bulletin boards
6 Shoot ___ breeze (chat)
9 Happiness
12 Expect
13 ___ and vinegar (salad dressing)
14 Ginger ___
15 Sharp and tangy
16 Crunchy snacks
18 Give a hand
20 Was in front of
21 Nickname of President Lincoln
23 Hearing organ
25 Cords
29 Animals that have calves
31 Peak
33 City in Nevada
34 Stand that an artist uses
36 Drink that sounds like a letter of the alphabet
38 Commercials
39 "It ___ a dark and stormy night"
41 Scheme
43 Crunchy snacks
47 What an active volcano may do
50 Word that can go in front of "glasses" or "lashes"
51 In a ___ (doing the same thing over and over)
52 Fix a shoelace that's come undone
53 ___ for mercy
54 "___ questions?"
55 One of the five senses

DOWN

1 Spinning character in Bugs Bunny cartoons, familiarly
2 In ___ of (amazed by)
3 Crunchy snacks
4 Toy that's fun to fly
5 Go out of ___ (become less hip)
6 "Only one ___ customer": 2 words
7 Small mountain
8 ___ Fudd (character in "Bugs Bunny" cartoons)
9 First month of the year: Abbreviation
10 Not new
11 "That's right!"
17 Stinky smell
19 Give someone a ___ on the back
21 Good card to have in the card game war

22 ___ constrictor (kind of snake)
24 Start to get moldy
26 Crunchy snacks
27 The last part
28 Letters that form a cry for help
30 Stitched
32 ___ talk (what a coach gives the team)
35 ___ Ingalls Wilder ("Little House on the Prairie" writer)

37 Red ___ (danger signal)
40 Amaze
42 ___ code (part of a phone number)
43 What a spider makes
44 How a sailor says "yes"
45 Part of a table
46 Where a pig lives
48 The center of a cherry
49 What a golfer puts the ball on

ACROSS

1 It forms on top of a wound
5 Janitors use them
9 First name of 3-Down
12 Part of a golf course
13 Tell ___ (don't tell the truth): 2 words
14 Astonishment
15 Ending for "respect"
16 Place, like on the internet
17 Amount at an auction
18 Ice cream flavor: 2 words
21 Shade of brown
22 It lives in a hive
23 Room in a prison
24 Ending for "count" or "baron"
25 ___ Biden (vice president from 2009 to 2017)
27 Separate using a baker's gadget
30 2,000 pounds
31 Music recordings, for short
34 Ice cream flavor: 2 words
38 X-___ vision (one of Superman's powers)
39 Direction on a compass
40 Green citrus fruit
41 Munched on
42 Not early
43 Last word of a prayer
44 What the P stands for in "MPH"
45 Moved quickly
46 Annoying person

DOWN

1 The long, thin part of an arrow
2 Snake that has a hood
3 Last name of the actor who was the voice of Buzz Lightyear
4 "Where have you ___?"
5 Makes potatoes ready for eating
6 Item in a Greek salad
7 Bread that has a pocket
8 Looked at
9 Kitchen furniture
10 Volunteer's reply to "Can someone help me?": 2 words
11 What an Olympic winner gets

19 One of the TV networks

20 Cubes that are in the freezer

24 "And on and on": Abbreviation

25 Wrote down in a hurry

26 Half of two

27 ___ heap (pile of junk)

28 "___ you!" ("You're not my friend anymore!"): 2 words

29 Area near the front door, in some houses

30 Try the food

31 Wind ___ (thing that hangs outside and makes jingly sounds)

32 Ten-cent coins

33 Used cash

35 Nighttime birds with big eyes

36 Jump

37 Applaud

ACROSS

1 "Get ___ my back!"
4 Joint near the middle of the body
7 Command a dog learns in obedience school
11 "America's Got Talent" judge ___ B
12 They go on kings or twos in the card game spit
14 State where Cincinnati is
15 "Prince ___" (song in the movie "Aladdin")
16 You go camping in one
17 Person who's not cool
18 Presses on a horn
20 "I'm ___ kidding!"
22 The Mediterranean ___
23 Prefix for "gravity" or "freeze"
24 Big structure in Egypt
26 Five-pointed thing
28 Important test
29 Home music systems
31 Health resorts
34 "___ says so?"
35 It's used to make roads
36 Copy of a magazine
37 ___ and rave (argue loudly)
39 Word that appears on the thing at 6-Down
41 Kind of poem (homophone for "owed")
42 Like the numbers 2, 4, and 6
43 Tools for gardeners
44 Tiny nibble
45 What a bird builds
46 Place for a pig
47 "Help us!"

DOWN

1 Big city in Nebraska
2 Criminal
3 Cartoon set in caveman times, with "The"
4 Head coverings
5 Put frosting on a cake
6 Small coin
7 Father's boy
8 Cartoon set in Springfield: 2 words
9 Showed on television, for example
10 Wise character in the "Star Wars" films
13 Shopping places

19 Toy for a windy day
21 What the Internal Revenue Service collects
24 "Practice what you ___!"
25 Boston's state: Abbreviation
27 Paintings and so on
29 Get rid of a beard
30 Cookies with white middles

32 Word that can go before "visual"
33 Oozes
34 Small brown bird
36 "The ___-Bitsy Spider"
38 Stuff that can cause an explosion: Abbreviation
40 A fisherman might throw it into the water

ACROSS

1 What keys fit into
6 "___ my pleasure"
9 Get at a store
12 Musical that includes the song "Tomorrow"
13 "How ___ you?"
14 Sly ___ fox: 2 words
15 Kriss Kringle's other name
16 Mother
17 Uncle ___ (symbol of America)
18 Word that might end a list: Abbreviation
20 Little ___ Muffet
22 Work in the movies
25 Big chunk of something
27 "I made a mistake!"
30 ___ of (in a way)
32 A while ___ (in the past)
33 Someone who isn't interesting
34 What the "little hand" points to
35 Some people pay it every month
37 "Do ___ Pass Go ..." (phrase in the game Monopoly)

38 It can go before "skirt" or "van"
40 You might get it pierced
42 ___ code (number at the end of an address)
44 Now ___ then
46 The end of one of Aesop's Fables
50 Great serve in tennis
51 Split ___ soup
52 Run away to get married
53 "___ out of here!"
54 Messy place
55 Did some stitching

DOWN

1 ___ Vegas
2 "I'm ___ roll!" ("Nothing is going wrong!"): 2 words
3 TV channel that shows mostly news
4 Toy that has a long tail
5 Chairs
6 "Do you know who ___?": 2 words
7 Orchestra instrument
8 Prefix for "finals" or "annual"

9 Orchestra instrument
10 Country formed in 1776: Abbreviation
11 Vegetable also called a sweet potato
19 Orchestra instrument
21 Weep loudly
22 What's left after something is burned
23 Sound a pigeon makes
24 Orchestra instrument
26 Number of years you've been around

28 ___ wrestling (John Cena's sport)
29 All ___ (ready to go)
31 Beginning for "cycle"
36 Makes less wild
39 Takes a short sleep
41 Part in a play
42 Zig and ___
43 Skating surface
45 24 hours
47 Pull on the oars
48 Monkey's big relative
49 Didn't follow

ACROSS

1 Small restaurant
5 Fast-moving card game
9 Received
12 "I cannot tell ___": 2 words
13 Very, very small
14 ___ de Janeiro, Brazil
15 Color of a carnation
16 Bring in the crops
17 Every last one
18 Enjoy a winter sport
19 ___-tac-toe
20 Possessed
22 Breaks free
25 Opposite of "subtract"
26 Wish
27 Surf and ___ (steak and seafood dinner)
29 ___ Baba
30 Take ___ measures (do something desperate)
33 Grin
35 "___ you kidding?"
36 A bolt fits into it
38 Wrestling hold
39 Desire
41 Truth or ___

42 Grow older
43 Border
44 Something ___ (not this)
45 Negative answers
46 Item planted in a garden
47 "Children should be ___ and not heard"

DOWN

1 Baseball players wear them
2 Similar
3 Ends of races: 2 words
4 What some people say when they see a mouse
5 Having a zebra design
6 Part of a jigsaw puzzle
7 One ___ million: 2 words
8 "Teh" instead of "the," for example
9 Big ending: 2 words
10 Applied grease to
11 Was a tattletale
19 Kind of dancing

21 What a frog supposedly can give you

23 Metal spring

24 Began

28 "___ only as directed"

29 Friend, in Spanish

31 Place for target practice

32 Say swear words

33 Have a short attention ___

34 They baa

37 Someone who's not 20 yet

40 Suffix for "lemon" or "Gator"

41 ___ Moines

ACROSS

1 Island country near Florida
5 Melt
9 Sticky stuff
12 Z ___ zebra: 2 words
13 Car
14 It might be pierced
15 Hairless
16 Member of the singing Chipmunks
18 Where Santa invites kids to sit
20 "Oh, ___ Pete's sake!"
21 One of the Seven Dwarfs
23 Direction where the sun rises
27 Assistant to Dr. Frankenstein
30 Sick
31 How you say "hello" and "goodbye" in Hawaii
33 Female sheep
34 Work for a newspaper or magazine
36 Cain's brother, in the Bible
37 Marry
38 At this very moment
40 Where a scientist works
42 "Batman" villain who says words like "purrrr-fect"
47 Light ___ (item in a lamp)

50 A long time ___ (in the past)
51 Red flower with sharp thorns
52 The world's largest continent
53 Ballpoint ___
54 Beef or pork, for example
55 All of those people

DOWN

1 Taxi
2 Its capital is Washington, D.C.: Abbreviation
3 He became president in 1993: 2 words
4 Cost an arm ___ leg: 2 words
5 "I tawt I taw a puddy ___!" (Tweety's saying)
6 "What did you say?"
7 Had a meal
8 Sound of a dog's bark
9 He became president in 2001: 3 words
10 It's used to paddle a canoe
11 State that's north of California: Abbreviation
17 "Where ___ go from here?": 2 words

19 Little vegetable found in a pod

21 Run out of battery

22 ___ Maid (card game)

24 Pie ___ mode (dessert with ice cream): 2 words

25 Cry

26 Jack-in-___-box

28 "I ___ you one!" ("Thanks for the help!")

29 One of the colors on the American flag

32 "Th-th-that's ___, folks!" (words from Porky)

35 Drag a car off the side of the road

39 Wiggly animal that you might use as fishing bait

41 Blind as ___: 2 words

42 What a baseball player wears on the head

43 How old a person is

44 One of the Three Stooges

45 Quiet ___ mouse: 2 words

46 It's in the middle of a tennis court

48 Say something that isn't true

49 Green ___ Packers (pro football team)

28

ACROSS

1 Used a chair
4 Agency that sends people into space: Abbreviation
8 Soup comes in these containers
12 "You ___ My Sunshine"
13 "That's just the way ___": 2 words
14 Kid on "The Andy Griffith Show"
15 False statement
16 Expensive property in the game Monopoly: 2 words
18 Puts in the mail
20 Long-___ (like Bugs Bunny)
21 Not to mention
22 Soft drink
25 Make an effort
26 ___ checkers (game with marbles)
29 ___ up (drink like a dog)
32 "Planet of the ___"
33 Cards that can be worth either 1 or 11 in blackjack
37 Edgar ___ Poe (famous American writer)
39 It holds a purse around a woman's shoulder
40 Expensive property in the game Monopoly

44 "What's the ___?" ("It doesn't matter anyway")
45 "Step ___!" ("Hurry!"): 2 words
46 Do as you're told
47 Christmas is in this month: Abbreviation
48 Baseball team from Cincinnati
49 What people catch butterflies in
50 Animal with large antlers

DOWN

1 You might dip nachos in this sauce
2 Name of the mermaid in "The Little Mermaid"
3 People older than 12 but younger than 20
4 Itty-bitty bites
5 "Now ___ theater near you!" (movie ad phrase): 2 words
6 What a private calls a sergeant, in the army
7 "___ a silly question, get a silly answer!"
8 Coke or Pepsi, for example
9 "I can't tell them ___" ("They look the same")
10 More pleasant

11 Like the inside of a watermelon
17 Round green vegetables
19 Friend of Sleepy and Grumpy
22 Drink through a straw
23 Word on a penny
24 ___ Moines (capital of Iowa)
27 You ball it up to make a fist
28 Have lunch
29 ___ Day (holiday in early September)
30 Without anyone else around
31 Clothing pattern that has different colors crossing each other
34 Gross, like belching at the table
35 Stand that's used to hold up a painting
36 Little bit of dust or soot
38 Martial ___ (karate, judo, etc.)
39 "The ___ the limit!" ("We can do anything!")
41 Took first place
42 Nickname for President Lincoln
43 Allow

ACROSS

1 Batman and Superman wear them
6 "To boldly go where no man ___ gone before" ("Star Trek" line)
9 It's similar to jelly
12 Ring ___ (sound familiar): 2 words
13 Covered with frozen water
14 Long ___ (in the past)
15 Soft drink that competes with Coke
16 "Yes, ___" (way to agree with a man)
17 "Charlotte's ___" (book about a spider)
18 Name of a skunk in some cartoons
20 Stupid
22 Part of the foot
24 Opposite of "happy"
26 A woman might carry her money and makeup in it
29 Dumbo flapped these in order to fly
31 "You can't have your cake and eat it ___"
33 Hand out the cards
34 Metal suit worn by a knight
36 One of Santa's assistants
38 Cash machine outside a bank: Abbreviation

39 "Peekaboo, ___ you!": 2 words
41 A teacher sits behind one
43 Frying ___ (kitchen item)
45 What Noah built
47 Requires
50 Have a part in a play
51 "Cross my heart and hope to ___"
52 Christmas ___ (kind of song you hear in December)
53 It isn't "no" or "maybe"
54 Money used in Japan
55 "What I Did on My Summer Vacation," for example

DOWN

1 "Put on your thinking ___!"
2 Name of Bart Simpson's grandfather
3 Hard candies
4 "Or ___!" (part of a threat)
5 Stumbles
6 Not hers
7 Dangerous liquid found inside batteries

8 You pour it on pancakes

9 Hard candies

10 "Act your ___ and not your shoe size!"

11 Crowd of people

19 Chow down

21 Pigs roll around in it

22 Drink that's popular in China

23 It makes a canoe move

25 Female deer

27 Stopped standing

28 Kind of tree

30 Letters that mean "help me!"

32 Ancient

35 "___ or not, here I come!"

37 It might surround a yard

40 One of the five Great Lakes

42 Large bodies of water

43 ___ attention (listen carefully)

44 "___ Ventura, Pet Detective"

46 Barbie's friend

48 "___ good turn daily" (Boy Scout slogan): 2 words

49 ___ as a fox (very sneaky)

ACROSS

1 Gets older
5 It might be parked in a garage
8 Touches softly
12 "Pleased to ___ you!"
13 "It's no ___!" ("It won't work!")
14 Thought
15 Large body of water on the east coast of America: 2 words
18 Part of the body that has a nail
19 Liquid inside a pen
20 Opposite of "hired"
23 Big relative of a monkey
24 Month before June
27 Cards that are sometimes better than kings
28 Dessert that has a crust
29 Opening in a fence
30 Homer's neighbor, on "The Simpsons"
31 Container for jelly
32 Squares of glass in a window
33 "___ Got the Whole World in His Hands"
34 What's on the skin of a bear or cat
35 Large body of water in Utah: 3 words
42 Incorrect way to say "isn't"

43 Christmas ___ (December 24)
44 Flower that has the same name as a part of the eye
45 Peas grow in them
46 Mediterranean ___ (large body of water)
47 Penny

DOWN

1 Question-and-answer session on Reddit, for short
2 "___ out of here!" ("Leave!")
3 Long, skinny fish
4 United ___ of America
5 Adorable
6 "Do ___ tell you!": 2 words
7 List of instructions that a cook follows
8 Choose
9 It can follow "lemon" or "Gator" in names of drinks
10 Beverage made by Lipton
11 ___ Francisco, California
16 Wynken, Blynken, and ___ (characters in a poem)
17 Nine minus eight

20 ___ mail (letters sent to famous people)

21 Cubes you can find in a freezer

22 Main color of a stop sign

23 People breathe it

24 Grown-up boy

25 Had a snack

26 "Uh-huh"

28 Doesn't fail a class in school

29 Food that can make your breath stink

31 Fast airplane

32 "I can't ___ up with this any longer!"

33 "The 500 ___ of Bartholomew Cubbins" (Dr. Seuss book)

34 Little insect that might bother a dog

35 Space between two teeth

36 ___ Grande (Texas river)

37 From beginning to ___

38 Illinois ___ (space in Monopoly): Abbreviation

39 "Just who do you think you ___?"

40 Family members

41 Ending for "small" that makes it mean "most small"

31

ACROSS

1 The fourth planet from the sun

5 Does a dance that makes "click" sounds with the shoes

9 Hobo

12 Bunches: 2 words

13 Continent where India is

14 Pretty ___ picture: 2 words

15 What day, month, and year it is

16 Dr. Seuss book: 2 words

18 You wipe your feet on it before entering a house

20 Room that might have a TV

21 Former vice president Quayle

24 "You're ___ the boss of me!"

26 You twist these in order to open some bottles

30 Dr. Seuss book: 3 words

34 Hit a ___ (run into problems)

35 Brown beverage

36 Animal in a dairy

37 Fuel for a car

40 A vain person might have a big one

42 Dr. Seuss book: 3 words

46 ___ Le Pew (cartoon skunk)

50 Lamb's mother

51 Voicemail prompt

52 Like the numbers 2, 4, and 6

53 What you hit a badminton birdie over

54 Part of a constellation

55 Geeky person

DOWN

1 Magazine featuring Alfred E. Neuman

2 State next to Georgia: Abbreviation

3 Decay

4 Long, skinny part of a flower

5 Art on a person's skin

6 One of the Pokémon trainers

7 The ___ Piper of Hamelin

8 When a store lowers its prices

9 Candy ___ (sweet treat)

10 The country south of Canada: Abbreviation

11 Name of the Grinch's dog

17 "___ upon a time ..."

19 "Baa baa black sheep, have you ___ wool?"

21 ___ and don'ts

22 Raggedy ___ (kind of doll)
23 LeBron James's sports organization: Abbreviation
25 It causes explosions: Abbreviation
27 Start of the alphabet
28 Athlete who gets paid
29 Carpenter's cutting tool
31 Brand of frozen waffles
32 Further away from the shallow end of the pool
33 Zig and ___
38 Insects that like picnics

39 "X marks the ___" (treasure map's phrase)
41 Not closed
42 "The Little Red ___" (story)
43 What the O in I.O.U. stands for
44 Dog, cat, or hamster, for example
45 Go ___ diet (try to lose weight): 2 words
47 Adam's partner, in the Bible
48 Miles ___ hour (how a car's speed is measured)
49 Finish

32

ACROSS

1 Dog's hand
4 Jack and ___
8 Pieces of wood that are put in a fireplace
12 Country between Canada and Mexico: Abbreviation
13 Dog in the comic strip "Garfield"
14 "___ what you mean" ("That makes sense"): 2 words
15 Bird that can be taught to talk
17 Food that contains meat, potatoes, and other vegetables
18 "The Princess and the ___" (fairy tale)
19 Rip
21 You might use it to keep wrapping paper in place
24 State whose capital is Carson City: Abbreviation
25 What the bride and groom say to the person marrying them: 2 words
28 It keeps your drink cold
29 Be ___ of (know about)
31 Chili ___ carne
32 It's filled with ink
33 Where you put your napkin when you eat

34 "There was an old woman who lived in a ___"
35 Tiger Woods plays this sport
37 ___-tac-toe
39 Twirled around
41 Pink bird with long legs
46 Name of the prince in "The Little Mermaid"
47 Where Aladdin's genie lived
48 ___ and arrow (what you use in archery)
49 "Don't use that ___ with me!" (parent's warning)
50 Parts of the face
51 Had some food

DOWN

1 Young dog
2 White ___ sheet: 2 words
3 Card game for two people
4 It ends with a punch line
5 Thought
6 "I cannot tell a ___"
7 You put it in an envelope
8 One of Bart Simpson's sisters
9 The largest bird in the world
10 "___ whiz!"

11 Use a needle and thread

16 Bigger relative of a monkey

20 Adam and ___

21 Money that's left for the waiter

22 Card with a single spot on it

23 Black-and-white bird

24 Sleep for a little while

26 Scooby-___

27 "___ nation under God, indivisible ..." (part of the Pledge of Allegiance)

29 Everything

30 Square breakfast food

34 Biology or physics, for example: Abbreviation

36 ___ in a while (sometimes)

37 Not wild

38 Bratty kids

39 "Ready, ___, go!"

40 Athlete who isn't an amateur

42 "Now I ___ me down to sleep ..."

43 The Los Angeles Lakers are in this group: Abbreviation

44 "You've ___ to be kidding!"

45 Have debts

ACROSS

1 Shut a door noisily
5 ___ and forth
9 Sounds that come after "tra" in a song: 2 words
10 Have a sore muscle
11 What candles are made of
14 Take ___ (sleep for a little while): 2 words
15 Lima ___ (kind of vegetable)
16 Butter ___ (flavor of Life Savers)
17 Revolutions ___ minute (what RPM stands for, on a record)
18 Opposite of "west"
19 Nick at ___ (what Nickelodeon calls its evening programs)
20 Spread messily, as finger paints
22 Summer is one
24 Music sometimes comes on them: Abbreviation
25 Fire ___ (insect that stings)
26 Places where you go bowling
29 Makes a sketch
31 Animal that roars

32 Bumper ___ (amusement park vehicles)
34 ___ up (misbehave)
36 "Monsters, ___" (animated movie)
37 You might skip it on a playground
38 "Twinkle, Twinkle, Little ___"
39 What some people say if they see a mouse
40 A flower, or a part of the eye
41 Measure of land
42 Things that you toss the rings over when you're playing ringtoss
43 "This is fun!"

DOWN

1 Smack in the face
2 A highway sometimes has four of them
3 Timer that wakes people up: 2 words
4 You might use one in a treasure hunt
5 Elephant whose wife's name is Celeste
6 Good cards to have in poker
7 Has a conversation

8 Boyfriend of Barbie

11 Timer that's worn on the arm

12 It might go before "biography" or "mobile"

13 Comic-book group that includes Wolverine and Cyclops: Hyphenated

18 Not difficult

19 The dog in "Peter Pan"

21 Where Adam and Eve lived

23 A basset hound has long ones

26 "I cannot tell ___" (what George Washington said): 2 words

27 Finish ___ (where runners end a race)

28 The number of points each team has

29 Gown

30 Frighten

33 Eat like ___ (wolf your food down): 2 words

35 Thing you'd find in a forest

37 Tear

38 Tool used by carpenters

34

ACROSS

1 ___-up (kind of shot in basketball)
4 What a parent might tell you to clean up
8 "When ___ your age ...": 2 words
12 "How was ___ know?": 2 words
13 Plenty: 2 words
14 Square piece with a letter on it, in the game Scrabble
15 "I need help!"
16 Curved roof on top of some sports stadiums
17 Nasty food given to pigs
18 The last word in a prayer
20 Kind of fruit
22 "You are what you ___"
23 What someone tells you to do when they're taking your picture
25 Imitated a cow
27 Put frosting on a cake
28 Beginning of the alphabet
29 Sirloin or T-bone
31 You sweep with it
33 Relative of a gorilla
34 Common answer to the question, "How are you?"
36 Body parts that blink

38 Not great, just okay: Hyphenated
40 Shredded paper with your hands
42 What people shout to encourage a bullfighter
43 Country in the Middle East
44 Female animals that have wool
45 2,000 pounds
46 "Look ___ when I'm talking to you!": 2 words
47 Rests on a bench
48 Stopping place

DOWN

1 One of the Simpsons
2 Tiny particles that all things are made of
3 He chased that "flea-bitten varmint" Bugs Bunny: 2 words
4 Furious
5 Run away and get married
6 More than none, but not all
7 What boiling water turns into
8 "___ a miracle!"
9 He chased the Road Runner: 3 words

10 "That's ___ off my mind!": 2 words

11 Labor Day is in this month: Abbreviation

19 "Have a ___ day!"

21 Sound a lion makes

24 It falls off a tree in autumn

26 Long, skinny musical instrument

29 Football or baseball, for example

30 You fly them in the air on windy days

31 Kind of cap worn by a French person

32 Cantaloupe is this type of fruit

33 Continent that China is in

35 "___ get it!" ("This finally makes sense!"): 2 words

37 Put in the mailbox

39 Number of horns on a unicorn

41 Suffix for "lion" or "count"

ACROSS

1 Dinner ___ movie (where some people go on dates): 2 words
5 Come out of a faucet very slowly
9 Male child
12 It helps hold a tree into the ground
13 State that's north of Missouri
14 Female who says "baa"
15 Candy with nuts in it: 2 words
17 Insect that might be eaten by an aardvark
18 Month after April
19 Put into storage
21 Sam-___ (character in "Green Eggs and Ham"): Hyphenated
24 Body part with a nail
26 Word on a triangular street sign
29 Food made from chopped-up cabbage
31 ___ up (totally finish)
33 Princess ___ ("Star Wars" character)
34 Offered a job to
36 Stay ___ (don't go anywhere)
38 Where a lion lives
39 Meat that comes from cows
41 Kanga's child, in "Winnie-the-Pooh"

43 "___ be a monkey's uncle!"
45 Candy with nuts in it: 2 words
50 Little wooden thing on a golf course
51 "Look before you ___"
52 Finished
53 Desperate cry for help
54 Not crazy
55 Observes

DOWN

1 Where your funny bone is
2 Neither here ___ there
3 Animal that barks
4 Part of a molecule
5 "What ___ say?" ("Please repeat that"): 2 words
6 Steal from
7 "As ___ saying ...": 2 words
8 Birthday ___ (celebration)
9 Plant that grows in the ocean
10 Possess
11 It can be used to catch a lot of fish at once
16 Grain that's sometimes used to feed horses

Crossword grid with numbered cells: 1, 2, 3, 4, 5, 6, 7, 8, 9, 10, 11 (row 1); 12, 13, 14 (row 2); 15, 16, 17 (row 3); 18, 19, 20 (row 4); 21, 22, 23, 24, 25, 26, 27, 28 (row 5); 29, 30, 31, 32, 33 (row 6); 34, 35, 36, 37, 38 (row 7); 39, 40, 41, 42 (row 8); 43, 44, 45, 46, 47, 48, 49 (row 9); 50, 51, 52 (row 10); 53, 54, 55 (row 11)

20 ___ and vinegar (salad toppings)

21 Suffix that means "sort of"

22 "___ Baba and the Forty Thieves"

23 Game played with small round objects

25 Supposedly, the "sixth sense": Abbreviation

27 ___ down (go to bed)

28 ___ Quayle (George Bush's vice president)

30 Tiny

32 Continent where France and Italy are

35 Hands out the cards

37 "It hit me like a ___ of bricks"

40 Insect that might bother a pet

42 Numbers that aren't evens

43 "___ about time!" ("Finally!")

44 Zodiac sign whose symbol is a lion

46 What a boy becomes when he grows up

47 Frank's brother, in the Hardy Boys books

48 Number said right before "liftoff!"

49 "You bet!"

36

ACROSS

1 Conceals
6 They try to sell things
9 Like two peas in a ___ (very similar)
12 Step ___ (move out of the way)
13 Permit
14 "In one ___ and out the other"
15 Where actors in a play are
16 Robert E. ___ (general in the Civil War)
17 Attempt
18 What's in ___ Head? (game involving the sense of touch)
20 Part of a book
22 "Rub-a-dub-dub, three men ___ tub": 2 words
24 Tool for a carpenter
26 Big
29 Toys that go around and around
31 What you give to a waiter
33 Rotate
34 What you sip a drink through
36 At this time
38 Peanut butter ___ jelly sandwich

39 "What's the big ___?" ("What do you think you're doing?")
41 Opposite of "rich"
43 "Peter ___"
45 "Last one in ___ rotten egg!": 2 words
47 Tools for scraping up leaves
50 "And so on": Abbreviation
51 Get ___ of (remove)
52 Actor Carell who voiced Gru in "Despicable Me"
53 "Golly!"
54 What you might call your father
55 Pitched

DOWN

1 "What ___ four wheels and flies?"
2 Ending for "novel" or "column"
3 Secret identity of Wonder Woman: 2 words
4 Border
5 They're planted in a garden
6 "___ aboard!"
7 Not shallow
8 What robbers do

9 Secret identity of Spider-Man: 2 words
10 It moves a rowboat along
11 Lacking moisture
19 Weekend day: Abbreviation
21 ___ station (place to get fuel)
22 "___ no big deal"
23 "Do ___ pass Go ..." (Monopoly instruction)
25 Finish in first place
27 ___ rummy (card game)
28 Dead-___ street
30 Depressed
32 "___ Goes the Weasel"
35 Strange
37 Most terrible
40 Japan is part of this continent
42 What a witness has to take, in the courtroom
43 It helps hold down a tent
44 Consumed
46 Find a sum
48 Cain and Abel's mother
49 Do some stitching

ACROSS

1 Speedy
5 Devices that electric guitars are attached to
9 Sound made by a woodpecker
12 The state where many Mormons live
13 It keeps a plant in the ground
14 "___ only as directed" (warning on medicine bottles)
15 Nevada city
16 Capital of South Carolina
18 Big brass instrument
20 Put ___ happy face (smile): 2 words
21 A lamb says it
23 Commercials
25 Destroys a balloon
29 Toymaker at the North Pole
30 Signs of sadness
33 Little white ___ (fib)
34 Like one end of a swimming pool
36 Peg used by Tiger Woods
37 "Are we having fun ___?"
38 Letters between Q and U
41 Old MacDonald had one
43 Capital of Hawaii

47 "I'll leave it ___ you" ("It's your decision"): 2 words
50 "You ___ here" (words on a mall map)
51 Dollar bills with George Washington on them
52 Made a knot
53 Moisture that forms on grass
54 You turn it in a book
55 Hour ___ (pointer on a clock)

DOWN

1 Mink coat, for example
2 Gobbled up
3 Capital of New Mexico: 2 words
4 Old-style word for "you"
5 Place with pinball machines and video games
6 Sound from a calf
7 Marco ___ (game played in a swimming pool)
8 Really surprise
9 You take a bath in it
10 "Do ___ say!": 2 words
11 Split ___ soup
17 It might show you how to find a treasure

19 The only mammal that flies
21 Where you sleep
22 Ginger ___ (bubbly drink)
24 "Little Miss Muffet ___ on a tuffet ..."
26 Capital of Washington
27 Chocolate cream ___ (kind of dessert)
28 ___ the table (get ready for dinner)
31 Say no
32 "Under the ___" (song in "The Little Mermaid")
35 Expert
39 It's fed to pigs
40 Fish that's sometimes used for sandwiches
42 Babe ___ (famous baseball player)
43 "I've ___ it up to here!" ("I'm fed up!")
44 Valuable stuff that miners find
45 Original
46 Drumstick
48 Five times two
49 Kind of strange

38

ACROSS

1 "Well, ___ be darned!"
4 ___ Diego, California
7 ___ hygiene (brushing one's teeth)
11 "Have a ___" ("Use this chair")
13 Prefix that means "the environment"
14 ___ stick (bouncy toy)
15 Harry Potter's school
17 Mates of rams
18 Homophone for "oh"
19 High social rank in England
21 "Do you know who ___?": 2 words
24 An exterminator might kill it
26 Your fingers and toes have them
29 Disease that people often get in the winter
30 24-___ gold
32 "That's ___ funny!"
33 People put chemicals in their swimming pools and aquariums to help get rid of this
35 ___ Wednesday (time before Easter)
36 Wise ___ (smart aleck)
37 Sudden burst of wind
39 British people drink a lot of it
41 Freezing

43 She's one of Harry Potter's best friends
48 "You're the only ___ can trust": 2 words
49 In the past
50 Gives a massage
51 El ___, Texas
52 1, 2, and 3, for example: Abbreviation
53 The sound a woodpecker makes on a tree

DOWN

1 Suffix that means "kind of"
2 Sign of the zodiac
3 Jet ___ (what people get when they fly from one time zone to another)
4 One of the tennis-playing Williams sisters
5 Be in a play
6 Where your nostrils are
7 "Carmen" is a famous one
8 Last name of Harry Potter's creator
9 Middle ___ (when people aren't young or old)
10 ___ Angeles
12 Number of people in a duo

1	2	3	■	■	4	5	6	■	7	8	9	10
11			12	■	13			■	14			
15				16				■	17			
■	■	■	18			■	19	20			■	■
21	22	23	■	24		25	■	26			27	28
29			■	30			31		■	32		
33			34		■	35			■	36		
■	■	37			38	■	39		40		■	■
41	42			■	43	44				45	46	47
48				■	49			■	50			
51				■	52			■	53			

16 Stops sleeping
20 "The Star-Spangled Banner" is the national ___
21 "___ tree falls in the forest, does it make a sound?": 2 words
22 100%
23 What Harry Potter calls non-magical people
25 "___ la la" (sounds in a song refrain)
27 "Skip to My ___"
28 Where a boar and sow might be
31 Houston's baseball team

34 Word that sometimes goes before "visual"
38 "Better late ___ never"
40 ___ conditioning
41 Short word for a police officer
42 Put ___ happy face (smile): 2 words
44 A conceited person has a big one
45 ___ of this world (really great)
46 Dwyane Wade plays in this group: Abbreviation
47 Supposed ability to read minds: Abbreviation

39

ACROSS

1 Touches softly
5 Like a giant
9 Sticky stuff that comes from a tree and is used to make syrup
12 Busy as ___: 2 words
13 Notion
14 What Spanish people shout at a bullfight
15 The ___ Ranger (Tonto's friend)
16 A cat says it
17 U.S. government spy agency: Abbreviation
18 Religious men who take vows of poverty
20 More likable
22 What you might do on the side of a mountain
23 Party thrower
27 Places where lions live
28 Person who watches a sports event
31 Walk back and forth, back and forth
33 Printing mistake, like "teh" instead of "the"
34 Thing on a shark's back
37 All by oneself
39 State that's next to New Hampshire
41 Letters between R and V
42 Sea animal that's used as an ingredient in chowder
46 Most tables have four of them
47 Black stuff used for paving roads
48 The March ___ ("Alice in Wonderland" character)
49 The opening in a piggy bank that you put the coins into
50 Paintings, sculptures, etc.
51 Not shut
52 ___ and ends (various things)

DOWN

1 Coconuts grow on these trees
2 "I can read you like ___!": 2 words
3 Where Novak Djokovic plays his sport: 2 words
4 Hide and ___
5 ___ Kaine (Hillary Clinton's running mate)
6 It can come after "Gator" or "lemon"
7 Sign of the zodiac whose symbol is a lion
8 Grassy area that has to be mowed
9 Where Carli Lloyd plays her sport: 2 words
10 Someone from another planet

11 Certain fruits

19 "___ sells seashells by the seashore" (tongue twister)

21 "What did ___ wrong?": 2 words

24 The month that Halloween is in: Abbreviation

25 Another word for 29-Down

26 Gently touch someone on the shoulder

29 Place where a pig lives

30 ___ Brady (quarterback of the New England Patriots)

31 Spaghetti and macaroni are this kind of food

32 Place in a church where people get married

35 "___ we trust" (phrase on all U.S. money): 2 words

36 Robins' homes

38 A sound that you hear again after you say it

40 Too

43 You form one when you sit down

44 "What ___ you talking about?"

45 Guys

ACROSS

1 Someone who looks down on other people
5 Money
9 ___-Man (video game character who eats dots)
12 The daughter of Hägar the Horrible, in comics
13 ___ code (the first part of a phone number)
14 The last word in the Pledge of Allegiance
15 "Look ___ from my point of view": 2 words
16 Building where grain is made into flour
17 ___ Grande (famous river)
18 Tony the Tiger's cereal: 2 words
21 The first two-digit number
22 Portland is a city in this state: Abbreviation
23 Hair on a horse's neck
24 Black-eyed ___ (little vegetable)
25 Pig farmer's enclosure
27 Plus
30 Homophone of "eight"
31 "Who Wants to ___ Millionaire": 2 words
34 Cereal with a honey taste: 2 words
38 "What do I ___ you?" ("How much money do I have to pay?")

39 Al ___ (Bill Clinton's vice president)
40 What poison ivy might make you do
41 Father of Rod and Todd Flanders, on "The Simpsons"
42 "Halt! Who ___ there?" (what a guard might say)
43 "My country, 'tis of ___ ..."
44 100 of them make a century: Abbreviation
45 What you get when you ask for change for a five-dollar bill
46 Looks at

DOWN

1 The long, thin part of an arrow
2 "The Hunchback of ___ Dame"
3 Vegetable that makes people cry when they peel it
4 Kibbles 'n' ___ (brand of dog food)
5 What a photographer uses
6 Go for ___ (travel by car): 2 words
7 ___-centered (vain)

8 One of the rooms in the board game Clue

9 Jacket that has a hood

10 Martian, for example

11 "___ but no cigar!"

19 Tic-tac-___

20 ___ Adams (actress who played Lois Lane in "Batman v Superman")

24 What the vegetable at 24-Across comes in

25 What you feel when there's a lot of pressure on you

26 Drink that's made from leaves

27 Extreme suffering

28 Further down

29 Vehicles that are pulled by dogs in some races

30 Have the same opinion as someone else

31 Clean oneself

32 The person who introduces other speakers at an assembly

33 What's left after something is burned

35 "Leggo my ___!" (frozen waffles' ad slogan)

36 Time for lunch

37 What baseball batters try to get

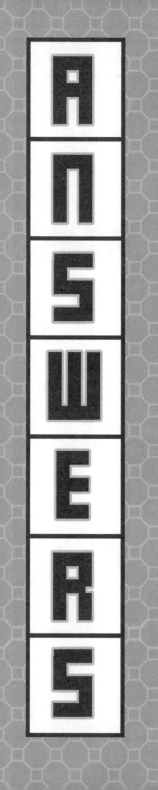

1

	P	O	P		P	E	A		T	E	A
	P	A	N	E		I	L	L		H	R	S
V	I	C	E	P	R	E	S	I	D	E	N	T
A	P	E	S		A	C	E		A	S	I	A
T	E	D		T	I	E		S	T	E	E	R
			S	O	N		P	I	E			
B	U	T	T	E		G	O	T		R	A	W
I	S	E	E		W	A	R		P	O	L	E
T	H	E	W	H	I	T	E	H	O	U	S	E
T	E	N		A	R	E		I	N	T	O	
Y	R	S		Y	E	S		D	Y	E		

2

J	A	Y	S		P	A	L		E	G	G	S
O	R	E	O		I	C	E		A	R	I	A
B	E	L	L		N	E	T		R	A	N	G
		L	A	S	T		T	E	N	N		
S	H	O	R	T		H	E	R		D	O	G
H	O	W		O	P	E	R	A		C	U	E
Y	E	S		V	A	N		S	M	A	R	T
			T	H	E	N		R	E	I	N	
S	H	O	O		A	P	E		T	Y	P	E
H	A	N	G		M	A	N		T	O	E	S
E	Y	E	S		A	N	T		S	N	A	P

3

A	B	E	L		O	N	A		S	H	E
M	A	G	I	C		R	A	T		T	O	Y
A	N	G	E	L		A	G	O		E	W	E
			S	I	G	N		P	A	R		
A	B	C		M	E	G		L	E	T	S	
R	O	O	T	B	E	E	R	F	L	O	A	T
M	O	V	E		J	O	E		S	P	Y	
			E	N	D		U	T	A	H		
B	A	R		A	L	I		S	A	L	A	D
O	R	E		D	E	C		T	R	A	C	E
B	E	D		S	E	E		D	Y	E	S	

4

H	U	M		P	O	E	T		B	Y	T	E
I	N	A		I	D	E	A		R	A	I	L
M	O	N	O	P	O	L	Y		A	H	E	M
			H	E	R		L	I	N	T		
I	N	T	O			P	O	T		Z	A	P
T	O	W		S	T	A	R	S		E	W	E
A	S	I		K	I	D			J	E	E	P
			S	H	I	N		G	O	O		
P	E	T	E		S	C	R	A	B	B	L	E
E	V	E	R		E	D	I	T		B	O	Y
W	E	R	E		L	E	N	S		S	U	E

5

	A	N	T		F	A	T		B	A	G
D	R	A	W		T	A	M	E		A	G	O
R	E	M	O	T	E	C	O	N	T	R	O	L
O	N	E		W	E	T	S		H	O	O	D
P	T	S		I	N	S		S	E	N	D	
			I	C	Y		W	H	Y			
	C	U	T	E		P	E	A		C	O	W
O	H	N	O		S	L	A	P		A	P	E
M	I	C	R	O	W	A	V	E	O	V	E	N
I	L	L		C	A	N	E		R	E	N	T
T	E	E		T	N	T		E	S	S		

6

L	O	B	E		L	A	C	E		F	A	N
I	L	A	Y		A	M	A	N		R	I	O
M	I	K	E		V	E	S	T		E	S	S
E	V	E		S	A	S	H		O	N	L	Y
	E	D	I	T		S	E	A	N	C	E	
		P	O	E	M		W	I	T	H		
	T	O	U	P	E	E		L	O	F	T	
W	I	T	S		N	A	P	S		R	E	N
I	M	A		C	A	S	E		F	I	N	E
M	E	T		A	C	E	S		L	E	S	S
P	R	O		B	E	L	T		U	S	E	S

7

```
I L L   O F F   B A R B S
T E A   T U B   A L O O K
S T P A T R I C K S D A Y
      H E S   L E O
F A V O R   J A R   N E T
A W A Y   N A P   L O V E
D E N   S E W   S I R E N
      W A R   R A P
A P R I L F O O L S D A Y
R A I S E   F A T   A L E
T Y P E S   A D S   M A T
```

8

```
P E T   S O S   R A B B I
O W E   E A T   A L L E N
P E A N U T S   L I O N S
      E S S   O P E N
W A D E S   B A H   D A Y
A C I D   P E R   D I N E
G E L   B A G   W E E D S
      B I L L   P A N
G E E S E   F O X T R O T
O G R E S   A G E   A R E
T O T E S   R O D   P E N
```

9

```
L A W   S C A N   B A I L
A G O   T A C O   E L M O
S E R P E N T S   A L P S
    L A P   C D S
L A D Y   B O A R   T I P
I T S   B U N N Y   A C E
T E E   A M E N   C R E W
    R E D     L O G
R A I N   S I D E W A Y S
U S E D   O V E N   M E A
B A S S   B E N D   E N D
```

10

```
J A B S   R A P   M A S T
I S E E   E S T   U T A H
F A N T A S I A   L A T E
    A M I   S P A
T I S   U S E   O N I O N
I N K   S T A R E   T W O
M A Y B E   R O T   S E W
    A D S   A I M
W A R M   H E R C U L E S
A R A B   I V E   L A S T
S E M I   N E D   E Y E S
```

11

```
  S C A R   H I P   W E B
S H A P E   O R E   A L A
L I N E N   M O N S T E R
A N T S   K E N   P E C K
P E A   A I R   P A R T
    L A S T   F A R M
  R O C K   T A N   E L F
T O U R   P I N   F L E E
E M P E R O R   A L O N E
L E E   A G E   M E N D S
L O S   N O D   P A S S
```

12

```
T I E S           C R I B
S T R E A K   K A R A T E
P A N A M A   O B E Y E D
      T I N   A C E
L A B S   G A L   P O P E
A R E   A L A   W I N
S T E W   R I B   S L E D
      A G O   E A T
S T E R E O   A P A C H E
H O L M E S   R E L I E S
Y A M S           L A M P
```

13

```
B A L D   B A D   S E E D
I T O R   O L E   P A N E
B A S E B A L L C A R D S
      W A R   L A D
H A S   A D S   T E L L S
A T O P   S A D   S A I L
T E X A S   W E D   S P Y
      S U M   A I R
F O O T B A L L G A M E S
E R I E   T I E   C A G E
W E L L   H E R   E D G E
```

14

```
S A P S   F E W   C A T
C L U E   S O L E   A L E
A B L E   O U S T   T I E
B U S   H U L A   B E E S
  M E R I T   L E A R N
      A S H   V A N
  B R I S K   A R G U E
B R A N   O D D S   N A G
O A K   O R E O   K I T E
I V E   W E A R   I T E M
L E D   L A D   D E N S
```

15

```
B A B E   W A V Y   G E M
A R A T   E X A M   E A R
D E B T   T E N C E N T S
    Y E S         A G E
R O B   I R O N   G R I P
I D O   S A F E S   A S A
O D O R   G A T E   T A N
    M A D         A S I
I C E W A T E R   H O R N
N O R   M A Y I   O N T O
A D S   S P E D   O X E N
```

16

```
M A R S   A T A   C H A T
O H I O   R E N   L I S A
P A D S   C A T W O M A N
    D O I T   S E W
P A L   N I P   I N P U T
O L E   S C O U R   E S E
P A R K A   E N D   N A N
    A N D   L O N G
M R F R E E Z E   A U N T
R O L E   N O S   B I B S
S W A N   S O S   S N A P
```

17

```
L I S T   A P E S   B A T
A S I A   D A V E   A R E
N A N C Y D R E W   L E E
D I G   A S I N   P L A N
  D E E R   S T R E S S
      E N D   S A P
  K A N S A S   N E A R
P O L Y   M O O D   L O U
O R E   H A R D Y B O Y S
P E R   A G E D   O N C E
E A T   M E S S   B E E S
```

18

```
C A P S   A C T   J O B
A G A I N   B O W   O N A
R O L L E R C O A S T E R
    L E A   L I E
M D S   D I P   N E W E R
P O O F   N O T   D E W Y
H E L L O   T O M   B E E
    U P S   W A S
A M U S E M E N T P A R K
D O S   R O Y   H A S T E
O W E   A G E   T H E Y
```

19

```
D I G   A B C     B U L B
I N A   L A L A   I D E A
M A U R I C E S E N D A K
S I Z E   H A T E   E S E
  R E A D   T A R   R E D
    L E T     R I P
M A P   L O A   E A T S
A L A   T U B A   P I E D
R I C H A R D S C A R R Y
S K E E   S U I T   E V E
H E R S   L A S   D E S
```

20

```
R I P   P E G S   R A C E
O N E   O X E N   I L A Y
T A N   L I M O U S I N E
    P O E T   U S E
S T A R S   P T A   F E D
H O L E   H I S   S O A R
Y E S   F O G   P A R T S
    A I R   N A M E
S P O R T S C A R   V A N
H A L T   E A S T   E G O
E N D S   S T A Y   R E D
```

21

```
S A G S   E S P     A S A
E X I T   R A I L   G A G
W E R E   A N T E L O P E
    A P E S   T O E
O F F   T E N   E G G S
A R F   C R U S T   O A K
R Y E S   T E A   R B I
    I A M   A N D I
E L E P H A N T   A L S O
N E W   S M E E   S L A W
D I E   A D D   H A T E
```

22

```
T A C K S   T H E   J O Y
A W A I T   O I L   A L E
Z E S T Y   A L M O N D S
    H E L P   L E D
A B E   E A R   R O P E S
C O W S   T O P   R E N O
E A S E L   T E A   A D S
    W A S   P L A N
W A L N U T S   E R U P T
E Y E   R U T   R E T I E
B E G   A N Y   T A S T E
```

23

```
S C A B   M O P S   T I M
H O L E   A L I E   A W E
A B L E   S I T E   B I D
F R E N C H V A N I L L A
T A N   B E E   C E L L
    E S S   J O E
S I F T   T O N   C D S
C H O C O L A T E C H I P
R A Y   W E S T   L I M E
A T E   L A T E   A M E N
P E R   S P E D   P E S T
```

24

```
O F F   H I P   S T A Y
M E L   A C E S   O H I O
A L I   T E N T   N E R D
H O N K S   N O T   S E A
A N T I   P Y R A M I D
    S T A R   E X A M
S T E R E O S   S P A S
W H O   T A R   I S S U E
R A N T   C E N T   O D E
E V E N   H O E S   N I P
N E S T   S T Y   S O S
```

25

```
L O C K S ■ I T S ■ B U Y
A N N I E ■ A R E ■ A S A
S A N T A ■ M O M ■ S A M
■ ■ E T C ■ M I S S ■ ■
A C T ■ S L A B ■ O O P S
S O R T ■ A G O ■ B O R E
H O U R ■ R E N T ■ N O T
■ M I N I ■ E A R ■
Z I P ■ A N D ■ M O R A L
A C E ■ P E A ■ E L O P E
G E T ■ S T Y ■ S E W E D
```

26

```
C A F E ■ S P I T ■ G O T
A L I E ■ T I N Y ■ R I O
P I N K ■ R E A P ■ A L L
S K I ■ T I C ■ O W N E D
■ E S C A P E S ■ A D D
■ H O P E ■ T U R F ■
■ A L I ■ D R A S T I C
S M I L E ■ A R E ■ N U T
P I N ■ W A N T ■ D A R E
A G E ■ E D G E ■ E L S E
N O S ■ S E E D ■ S E E N
```

27

```
C U B A ■ T H A W ■ G O O
A S I N ■ A U T O ■ E A R
B A L D ■ T H E O D O R E
■ L A P ■ ■ F O R ■
D O C ■ E A S T ■ I G O R
I L L ■ A L O H A ■ E W E
E D I T ■ A B E L ■ W E D
■ N O W ■ ■ L A B ■
C A T W O M A N ■ B U L B
A G O ■ R O S E ■ A S I A
P E N ■ M E A T ■ T H E Y
```

28

```
S A T ■ N A S A ■ C A N S
A R E ■ I T I S ■ O P I E
L I E ■ P A R K P L A C E
S E N D S ■ ■ E A R E D
A L S O ■ S O D A ■ T R Y
■ ■ C H I N E S E ■ ■
L A P ■ A P E S ■ A C E S
A L L A N ■ ■ S T R A P
B O A R D W A L K ■ U S E
O N I T ■ O B E Y ■ D E C
R E D S ■ N E T S ■ E L K
```

29

```
C A P E S ■ H A S ■ J A M
A B E L L ■ I C Y ■ A G O
P E P S I ■ S I R ■ W E B
■ P E P E ■ D U M B ■
T O E ■ S A D ■ P U R S E
E A R S ■ T O O ■ D E A L
A R M O R ■ E L F ■ A T M
■ I S E E ■ D E S K ■
P A N ■ A R K ■ N E E D S
A C T ■ D I E ■ C A R O L
Y E S ■ Y E N ■ E S S A Y
```

30

```
A G E S ■ C A R ■ P A T S
M E E T ■ U S E ■ I D E A
A T L A N T I C O C E A N
■ ■ T O E ■ I N K ■ ■
F I R E D ■ A P E ■ M A Y
A C E S ■ P I E ■ G A T E
N E D ■ J A R ■ P A N E S
■ H E S ■ F U R ■
G R E A T S A L T L A K E
A I N T ■ E V E ■ I R I S
P O D S ■ S E A ■ C E N T
```

31

```
MARS  TAPS  BUM
ALOT  ASIA  ASA
DATE  THELORAX
   MAT  DEN
DAN  NOT  CAPS
ONBEYONDZEBRA
SNAG  TEA  COW
   GAS  EGO
HOPONPOP  PEPE
EWE  TONE  EVEN
NET  STAR  NERD
```

32

```
PAW  JILL  LOGS
USA  ODIE  ISEE
PARAKEET  STEW
    PEA  TEAR
TAPE  NEV  IDO
ICE  AWARE  CON
PEN  LAP  SHOE
   GOLF  TIC
SPUN  FLAMINGO
ERIC  LAMP  BOW
TONE  EYES  ATE
```

33

```
SLAM  BACK
LALA  ACHE  WAX
ANAP  BEAN  RUM
PER  EAST  NITE
 SMEAR  SEASON
   CDS  ANT
ALLEYS  DRAWS
LION  CARS  ACT
INC  ROPE  STAR
EEK  IRIS  ACRE
   PEGS  WHEE
```

34

```
LAY  MESS  IWAS
ITO  ALOT  TILE
SOS  DOME  SLOP
AMEN  PEAR  EAT
 SMILE  MOOED
   ICE  ABC
 STEAK  BROOM
APE  FINE  EYES
SOSO  TORE  OLE
IRAN  EWES  TON
ATME  SITS  END
```

35

```
ANDA  DRIP  SON
ROOT  IOWA  EWE
MRGOODBAR  ANT
   MAY  STOW
IAM  TOE  YIELD
SLAW  USE  LEIA
HIRED  PUT  DEN
   BEEF  ROO
ILL  ALMONDJOY
TEE  LEAP  DONE
SOS  SANE  SEES
```

36

```
HIDES  ADS  POD
ASIDE  LET  EAR
STAGE  LEE  TRY
  NEDS  PAGE
INA  SAW  LARGE
TOPS  TIP  SPIN
STRAW  NOW  AND
  IDEA  POOR
PAN  ISA  RAKES
ETC  RID  STEVE
GEE  DAD  THREW
```

37

F	A	S	T		A	M	P	S		T	A	P
U	T	A	H		R	O	O	T		U	S	E
R	E	N	O		C	O	L	U	M	B	I	A
		T	U	B	A		O	N	A			
B	A	A		A	D	S		P	O	P	S	
E	L	F		T	E	A	R	S		L	I	E
D	E	E	P			T	E	E		Y	E	T
			R	S	T		F	A	R	M		
H	O	N	O	L	U	L	U		U	P	T	O
A	R	E		O	N	E	S		T	I	E	D
D	E	W		P	A	G	E		H	A	N	D

38

I	L	L		S	A	N		O	R	A	L
S	E	A	T		E	C	O		P	O	G	O
H	O	G	W	A	R	T	S		E	W	E	S
			O	W	E		E	A	R	L	
I	A	M		A	N	T		N	A	I	L	S
F	L	U		K	A	R	A	T		N	O	T
A	L	G	A	E		A	S	H		G	U	Y
		G	U	S	T		T	E	A		
C	O	L	D		H	E	R	M	I	O	N	E
O	N	E	I		A	G	O		R	U	B	S
P	A	S	O		N	O	S		T	A	P

39

P	A	T	S		T	A	L	L		S	A	P
A	B	E	E		I	D	E	A		O	L	E
L	O	N	E		M	E	O	W		C	I	A
M	O	N	K	S		N	I	C	E	R	
S	K	I		H	O	S	T		D	E	N	S
		S	P	E	C	T	A	T	O	R	
P	A	C	E		T	Y	P	O		F	I	N
A	L	O	N	E		M	A	I	N	E	
S	T	U		C	L	A	M		L	E	G	S
T	A	R		H	A	R	E		S	L	O	T
A	R	T		O	P	E	N		O	D	D	S

40

S	N	O	B		C	A	S	H		P	A	C
H	O	N	I		A	R	E	A		A	L	L
A	T	I	T		M	I	L	L		R	I	O
F	R	O	S	T	E	D	F	L	A	K	E	S
T	E	N		O	R	E		M	A	N	E	
		P	E	A		S	T	Y			
A	L	S	O		A	T	E		B	E	A	
G	O	L	D	E	N	G	R	A	H	A	M	S
O	W	E		G	O	R	E		I	T	C	H
N	E	D		G	O	E	S		T	H	E	E
Y	R	S		O	N	E	S		S	E	E	S

ABOUT THE AUTHOR

TRIP PAYNE is a professional puzzle constructor and editor from Los Angeles, California. He made his first puzzles when he was in elementary school, had his first puzzle in a national magazine when he was in high school, and worked for a major puzzle magazine when he was in college. He has made kids' puzzles for such places as *Scholastic News*, *Games Junior*, and *TV Guide*. You can visit his website at tripleplaypuzzles.com and follow him on Twitter @PuzzleTrip.